Winning by TEAMWORK

Written by Kelli L. Hicks

Content Consultant
Taylor K. Barton, LPC
School Counselor

Rourke
Educational Media

rourkeeducationalmedia.com

Scan for Related Titles
and Teacher Resources

www.rourkeeducationalmedia.com

PHOTO CREDITS: Cover: © Hero Images; page 4, 6:, 22 © Steve Debenport; page 5, 10: © kali9; page 7: © fstop123; page 8: © Denys Kurbatov; page 9: © PCN/Corbis; page 11: © Library of Congress; page 12: © Jeff Haynes; page 13: © Amy Myers; page 14: © Lorraine Swanson; page 15: © Michael Pettigrew; page 16, 17: © Cynthia Farmer; page 18: © Carmen Martínez Banús; page 19: © Associated Press; page 20, 21: © Andrew Rich

Edited by Precious McKenzie

Cover and Interior Design by Tara Raymo

Library of Congress PCN Data

Winning By Teamwork / Kelli L. Hicks
(Social Skills)
ISBN 978-1-62169-903-3 (hard cover) (alk. paper)
ISBN 978-1-62169-798-5 (soft cover)
ISBN 978-1-62717-009-3 (e-Book)
Library of Congress Control Number: 2013937298

Rourke Educational Media
Printed in the United States of America,
North Mankato, Minnesota

Also Available as:

rourkeeducationalmedia.com

customersevice@rourkeeducationalmedia.com • PO Box 643328 Vero Beach, Florida 32964

TABLE OF CONTENTS

WHAT DOES IT TAKE TO WIN?

What does it take to win a game? When you pass the ball, someone has to be there to receive it. You need teammates that you can rely on to get the job done. In order to win, you must have **teamwork**.

DO WE THINK ALIKE?

What makes a team successful? A team shares a **vision**. They believe in the same ideas and **principles**. They work together, all the time.

The same advice applies to school groups or sports teams. When all the members of a team set the same goals and agree on how to meet those goals, everyone understands what has to happen for the team to win.

If you practice with 100% effort and intensity, it will have a great impact on your performance in a competition or game.

Team members share **responsibility**. Each member has to do his or her best to contribute. Every single member of the team impacts the game. If each player tries to do their best all the time, then your team will have a better chance of succeeding.

The U.S. Women's Gymnastics team won the team gold medal during the 2012 Olympics. Each woman on the team has her own unique strengths but they came together through teamwork to succeed!

COMMUNICATION IS KEY

Great teams **communicate**. Talking about what is happening in the game and listening to ideas that can make the team better are important to the success of the team.

"The way a team plays as a whole determines its success. You may have the greatest bunch of individual stars in the world, but if they don't play together, the club won't be worth a dime." –Babe Ruth

Members of a team cheer for each other and support each other. Always stay in control of your emotions and be positive. One negative **attitude** can affect the whole team and destroy your team's chances of doing well.

Team members help each other even when times are tough. The Louisville Cardinals men's basketball team supported Kevin Ware after he severely injured his leg during the playoffs. The team went on to win the 2013 NCAA men's basketball championship.

Louisville Cardinals

You can show you believe in your teammates by cheering for them and reminding them to do their best.

SPORTSMANSHIP

The score of the game doesn't always go in your favor. Strong teams encourage each other, even when times are tough. You have to stick together during the good and the bad times. You won't win every game, but at least you can have a winning attitude.

penalty

Home

8:02

Guests

1

3

period 3

Don't let poor behavior from others affect your team. Always be a good sport, no matter what the scoreboard says. If your team loses, congratulate the winning team and shake their hands. Maybe your team will win the next game.

Encourage your teammates to be the best they can be. When you do your best, others will too.

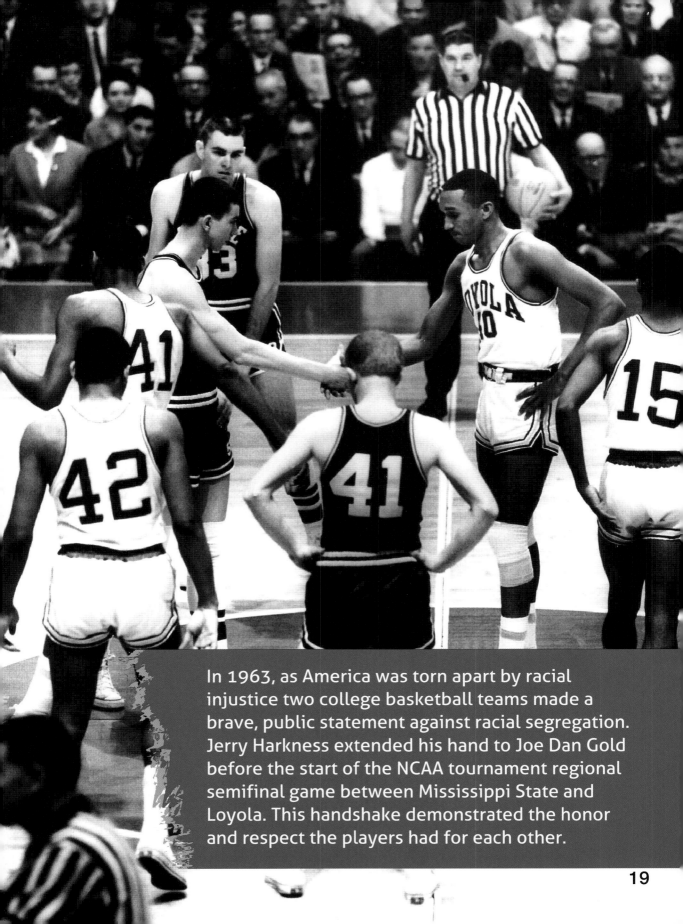

In 1963, as America was torn apart by racial injustice two college basketball teams made a brave, public statement against racial segregation. Jerry Harkness extended his hand to Joe Dan Gold before the start of the NCAA tournament regional semifinal game between Mississippi State and Loyola. This handshake demonstrated the honor and respect the players had for each other.

The opportunity to play sports is a **privilege**. Every team has a responsibility to honor, **respect**, and protect the game, and one another. For many professional athletes they must display good personal conduct, both on and off the field. Not only is it in their contracts and affects their pay, but it is the right thing to do.

As the challenges get harder, the need for teamwork increases. Strong teamwork makes winners, no matter what the scoreboard says.

GLOSSARY

attitude (AT-i-tood): your feelings about something that affects your behavior or mood

communicate (kuh-MYOO-ni-kate): to share information, ideas, or feelings with someone else

principles (PRIN-suh-puhlz): a basic truth, law, or belief

privilege (PRIV-uh-lij): a special right given to a person or group of people

respect (ri-SPEKT): a feeling of admiration or high regard for someone or something

responsibility (ri-SPAHN-suh-BIL-i-tee): a job or duty

teamwork (TEEM-wuhrk): working together with a group or team

vision (VIZH-uhn): an idea or plan

INDEX

WEBSITES TO VISIT

www.sikids.com

www.nflrush.com

www.exploratorium.edu/explore/staff_picks/sports_science

ABOUT THE AUTHOR

Kelli Hicks is a teacher and author who lives in Tampa, Florida, with her husband, her daughter Mackenzie, her son Barrett, and her golden retriever Gingerbread. Kelli is a soccer coach who knows all about the excitement of winning and the sorrow of defeat. She learns every week from her girls how to work as a team and how to support each other to overcome defeat. Go Lady Rangers!

Meet The Author!
www.meetREMauthors.com

24